# CHINA

*A Photographic Journey*

TEXT: **Bill Harris**

CAPTIONS: **Laura Potts**

PHOTOGRAPHY: **Colour Library Books Ltd.**

DESIGNED BY: **Teddy Hartshorn**

DIRECTOR OF PRODUCTION: **Gerald Hughes**

CLB 3003
© 1993 Colour Library Books Ltd., Godalming, Surrey, England.
All rights reserved.
This 1993 edition published by Crescent Books,
distributed by Outlet Book Company, Inc., a Random House Company,
40 Engelhard Avenue, Avenel, New Jersey 07001.
Printed and bound in Spain.
ISBN 0 517 07680 2
8 7 6 5 4 3 2 1

# CHINA

## A Photographic Journey

Text by
BILL HARRIS

**CRESCENT BOOKS**
**NEW YORK • AVENEL, NEW JERSEY**

In 1978, when it once again became possible for Westerners to visit China, 1.8 million people took advantage of the opportunity. By 1987, the number had swelled to 23.7 million, and the rate of growth doesn't show any signs of slowing down.

As though there wasn't enough for them to see and do, foreign visitors are lured by luxury cruises along China's coast, by newly-developed beach resorts and even an American-style amusement park. It is possible to pay for many things with credit cards, and if a visitor has trouble manipulating chopsticks, forks are available nearly everywhere. It is possible for Westerners to experience China without experiencing severe culture shock.

But no matter what other things they may have come to experience, every visitor makes it a point to see the Great Wall, ironically a symbol of China's historical effort to keep foreigners out. And no one who sees the wall for the first time is quite prepared for the experience. It is nothing more or less than the greatest man-made structure on the face of the earth. In some places it is wide enough for five cavalrymen to march side-by-side between its massive towers. It averages 21.5 feet high, and extends about 3,750 miles from the Bohai Gulf to the Gobi Desert. It was once nearly twice as long as it is today, but over the centuries, wind and rain have destroyed sections that held back the mighty armies of the north. In the 1970s, at least one long section was destroyed by Chinese soldiers who found it a handy source of stones to build a new military base. Those same soldiers were put to work rebuilding what they had torn down and found out for themselves what an incredible feat had been accomplished by the original builders.

Parts of the wall have been standing for almost 2,400 years. Yet China's great philosopher, Confucius, had been dead for more than 150 years when construction began. And he was the product of change in a thousand-year tradition that had existed before him.

There is no reliable history of the beginnings of Chinese culture. But the first dynasties, dating back to 2333 B.C., were said to have been headed by three successive wise kings. The first was Yao, who bequeathed his kingdom to one of his subjects, Shun, rather than his son. Shun did the same, but his successor, Yü, established the custom of hereditary rule. All three have been credited with almost supernatural powers, but their stories were handed down by word of mouth for nearly 2,000 years before written records were established.

The Shang Dynasty, established around 1751 B.C., was the first to record its exploits in writing, and is generally considered the beginning of Chinese history. Its kings were probably the first to establish walled cities. They are also believed to have been the first to be buried in elaborate tombs with animal and human sacrifices at their side.

The Shang kings expanded their territory in every direction. But the city-states they absorbed remained relatively independent of them. The center of power was far away and out of touch. At the height of Shang influence, the dynasty controlled about 30 states, each of which was in turn controlled by a lord whose only obligation was to provide soldiers in time of war, to send prescribed tributes to the capital and to honor the king as a supreme being. By the time the dynasty ended, the actual power of the king, even though he was considered almost a god, was already being eroded.

The Zhou Dynasty was able to unseat the Shangs partly by conspiring with the disloyal feudal lords. Its first king had to risk the same disloyalty by distributing the land among family clans and establishing a network of scattered garrisons to keep an eye on the people and the families that actually controlled them. The Zhou, who had come from the tribes of Tibet and Turkey, were careful to let the people maintain most of their old traditions and customs. They gradually added their own to the mixture and an entirely new culture grew from the marriage.

The people of the north, where heads of families officiated over religious rites, had never had a need for priests, who had been high in the order of things among the Shangs. When the conquerors absorbed the idea that the king was an intermediary between them and heaven, it was only natural that the Zhou king, as head of a symbolic family, was designated the supreme priest as well. But there was an obligation that went with it. The kings were well aware that if they didn't perform their ceremonial duties correctly, heaven would respond with a drought or a blizzard or some other manifestation of divine displeasure. They had put the Shang priests out of business, but they wisely kept them around as scholars and advisors.

The Zhou empire, said to have encompassed more than a thousand fiefdoms, was run from an imperial city near present-day Xi'an. It was considered the center of the universe, but the world outside was populated by hostile Turkish and Mongolian tribes. Eventually, the outsiders overran the capital and the center of the universe was shifted 200 miles eastward to Luoyang, in what has become Honan province.

The Zhou kings were safer from outside attack in their new capital, but their actual power didn't extend far beyond the city's walls. The far-off feudal lords continued to run their own affairs, but they needed a central figure to deal with heaven, the only thing they felt they couldn't control themselves. They were willing to leave that power in the hands of the king, and though it was considerable, it was the only real influence he had.

Most of the overlords paid little more than lip service to the man they called the Son of Heaven. Their real concern was with temporal affairs, and in the processs of consolidating their power, they gradually assimilated the customs of the people they controlled. The result was the creation of states with cultures all their own. The kings chose to think of many of their far-flung subjects as uncivilized barbarians, but in time at least one state, the important trading center of Qin, in what is now Shantung province, was more civilized than Luoyang itself. It was near there, and during its period of great power and wealth, that Confucius was born in 551 B.C.

The religious power of the king had elevated the status of the scholars by then. The overlords had come to rely on them to supervise their own rites and the court needed them to enhance the importance of the king. Confucius trained to become a scholar and worked as a teacher among the children of various noblemen. As such, he dealt directly with dozens of different feudal lords and began forming a philosophy related to their duties and obligations. He passed those ideas along to a large following of students and other scholars who joined him as he moved through the countryside. His teachings established a general moral code that still exists, though it has been downgraded in recent decades. Confucius enhanced the tradition that heaven guided the actions of men, but added the idea that heaven itself was bound to follow a set of rules. Harmony with those rules, as outlined by his philosophy, has been at the heart of Chinese thought ever since. He reminded his followers of their belief that the family unit was the model for all society and that the head of the unit was the eldest male. No two people were exactly equal, but each had a role to play, and everyone understood perfectly what that role was to be. The model extended all the way to the king, and through him to heaven itself. Such was the influence of Confucian thought that his ideas were to hold sway with every ruler after the Zhou Dynasty.

At about the same time Confucius was attracting a following, another philosopher, Lao Tzu, was also writing of the need for harmony with the laws of the universe, which he called Tao. The difference between the two men was not the goal – spiritual peace – but the route to attaining it. Confucius prescribed rules for life in communities and each person's role in society. Lao Tzu called for a withdrawal from the community and said that rules should be unnecessary, even for the king. Their ideas, an affirmation of the principles of the Zhou Dynasty, gave rise to an enduring set of attitudes that include a love of ritual, ancestor worship, a complex bureaucracy and the idea of yin-yang – the centerpiece of Chinese art and literature.

Yin-yang is a perceived force of opposites always interacting to produce harmony in nature. Each is thought to grow from the other and each alternately controls events. The universe, in the Chinese view, is constantly in motion and composed of interrelated forces, each following its own natural law. It is a theory that runs counter to the Western idea of a God who created the universe and may exert His will on all of nature. Even the introduction of Buddhism from India, Christianity from the West and refinements introduced by later Chinese philosophers have not changed the basic philosophical ideas of the Chinese people, which go further back in time than any other human belief.

The natural frontiers of China encourage self-sufficiency. China's eastern border is the vast Pacific Ocean. Impenetrable jungles isolate it from the south, and the Himalayan Mountains seal it off in the southwest. To the north and west are deserts and grasslands that stretch for hundreds of miles. For many centuries, visitors from any other part of the world who did cross the barriers were considered representatives of vassal states and subject to what the Chinese regarded as a civilizing influence. Up until the 19th century, foreigners were welcome only as long as they adopted Chinese customs, beliefs and dress. China considered itself the only center of culture in the world and the further from the center a foreigner lived, the more barbaric he was believed to be.

China's first major contacts with the outside world were made during the Han Dynasty, which began in 206 B.C. Its first emperor, Wu Ti, conquered the northern tribes and brought southern China under his control. His successors began protecting trade caravans from Central Asia and the Middle East. Han ambassadors established contact with the great Roman Empire, though each culture considered the other quite uncivilized and not worth the bother. Toward the end of the dynasty, merchants from India brought Buddhism to China. The upper classes hardly noticed, but it raised new questions about reincarnation, and the Buddhist belief that actions in this life are rewarded or punished in the next was a very attractive idea to the lower classes. Like every other foreign idea, the Indian religion was altered to fit the Chinese vision of the world. But it also altered China's vision of itself.

After the fall of the Han Dynasty, the country floundered for more than 500 years under a series of dynasties that divided the people as much as the Han had united them. Under the Tang Dynasty, beginning in 618 A.D., both Buddhism, which became the official state religion, and Confucianism, which provided the emperors with a tie to the past, became the means of reunifying the people. It marked a golden age for China, during which her armies took the Sinkiang basin from the Turks and brought Korea under their domination. At the same time they established a lucrative world trade, and China became a crossroads where foreigners, living undisturbed in their own enclaves, created new markets for China's silks, spices and precious metals. The caravans that served the merchants brought new influences into the culture and with them a flowering of poetry and literature. Painting and sculpture were also enhanced by foreigners, many of whom were brought in to decorate Chinese temples.

The Sung Dynasty, which followed in 960 A.D., was a period of great inventiveness, the time when the Chinese developed, among other things, movable type, gunpowder and the magnetic compass. It also marked a high point in the art of medicine and saw the introduction of a code of ethics for doctors. And during the same period, theories on judicial conduct and rights of the accused in court hearings were advanced far beyond anything that would be established in Western countries for hundreds of years. The arts flourished, too, and for the first time painters were given official recognition and status by emperors, one of whom, Hui Tsung, was one of the great art collectors of that or any other time.

During the more than 300 years of Sung influence, China's population topped 100 million, with the populace of some cities reaching a million, engendering severe overcrowding. Yet, while Europe languished in the Dark Ages, orphanages, nursing homes for the aged poor and state pharmacies were available in Chinese cities and paper money became legal tender. Between 850 and 1050 coal and iron consumption grew at faster rate than in England during the first two centuries of industrialization. Farming techniques were highly advanced and more than adequate to feed the people. For the first time in the history of the world, people were freed to produce commercial goods without the additional burden of growing food. It would be another five centuries before such development would revolutionize life in the West.

The Sung were driven from their northern territories after attacks by Mongol and Tatar tribes in 1126, yet the brother of the captured emperor managed to escape and established a new dynasty in the south with its capital at Hangzhou. Life for the upper classes went on much as before. Culture thrived, commerce boomed and the Mongols in northern China were held at bay through payment of tribute. Wealthy landowners, though, were hit with measures that confiscated land from the largest of them during this time in order to finance a defense against the impending invaders. Consequently, when the Mongols began casting lustful eyes on the southern territories, the gentry joined with them in hopes of saving their property. Their scheming paid off for them, but it opened the door for a new Mongol leader, Kublai Khan, the grandson of Genghis Khan, who completed the work of his infamous predecessor and swept away the Southern Sung Dynasty in 1279, bringing all of China under his control.

It was the first time in their history that the Chinese were ruled by outsiders, but the traditional gentry were allowed to keep their estates, and through them their power over the peasants. As others had before them, the new rulers took land from the peasants and then used them as forced labor, this time to build their magnificent new capital at Beijing. The site had been chosen for its nearness to Mongolia, but because it was far from the centers of food production, a network of canals had to be built, and peasants were recruited for that job as well. Over time, the number of taxpaying farmers was dramatically reduced. Foreign merchants were also welcomed with open arms, and among the inducements that lured them to China was a complete exemption from taxes. They were allowed to travel anywhere in the country in search of profits, which were then sent abroad. The Mongols, meanwhile, were building more elaborate palaces and temples and living in splendor, while the ordinary people were being exploited and forced to live in poverty, as well as virtual slavery.

The outside world, on the other hand, saw only the magnificence of the cities. Visitors like Marco Polo were enthusiastic in their reports and trade with the court of Kublai Khan became the goal of merchants in all parts of the West. But as trade increased, China itself slowly became impoverished. The arts flourished as before, but the progress in industrial technology that had held such promise for the future suddenly stopped. The Chinese view at the time was that once some idea was been perfected, it was just that – perfect – and so required no further consideration or development. This goes some way towards explaining the failure of the Chinese to develop their discoveries, but there are dozens of theories about what happened. Some say that it was simply because the population of China was so huge that the use of machines to replace human labor wasn't economical.

But the people who did the actual work were starving. In 1325 they began a series of uprisings in which they killed Mongols and native gentry as well. The rebels were held at bay for nearly a half century, though they continued to fight and their numbers kept increasing. They were led by Chu Yuan-chang, a peasant and former Buddhist monk, who was destined to become T'ai Tsu, the first emperor of the Ming. Over the next four decades they conquered all of the south and in 1368 they took Beijing without a struggle and established the Ming Dynasty with its capital at Nanjing.

T'ai Tsu attempted to limit power of the upper classes and passed new laws dividing the estates of the rich among the peasants. But there weren't the means of enforcing their laws, and the gentry, who had become the principal taxpayers, retained most of their power. The new ruler had also obviously been as impressed as foreigners had been with the splendor of Mongol Beijing, and set out to make the old capital more magnificent than ever. But to guard against Mongol encroachment on their northern borders, the Ming emperors were to move their capital back to the former Mongol city in 1421.

The influence of foreigners dwindled during the Ming years. Chinese citizens were forbidden to have contact with outsiders except under official control. The Great Wall was rebuilt and strengthened and the Chinese armies withdrew behind it. The rulers gave themselves absolute powers, but in spite of a virtual dictatorship, culture flourished once again. The era is remembered as one of the most important in Chinese literature, and especially for the creation of novels in colloquial language. Opera and other musical forms were perfected, and architectural styles that are still followed were developed under Ming influence. Porcelain was perfected during this time,

and the Ming vases made at this time are priceless collectors' items to this day. The ordinary people, too, thrived during the 276 years of Ming rule. Their standard of living, enhanced by new methods of production and farming, and relieved at last of the burden of slavery, was easily the highest of any people anywhere in the world.

But life at court seems to have been a little too good. As had happened before, the Ming emperors became corrupt, and members of their official families divided into cliques. Their intrigues took their attention away from what was going on outside the walls of the Forbidden City, and their old enemies, the Mongols, were more than willing to take advantage of the situation. In the 1630s, they joined forces with the Manchurians to defeat the Koreans and forged an alliance based on Chinese models to establish a new dynasty they called Qing, meaning "pure."

After the Imperial City fell to Chinese rebels in 1644, the Manchus arrived as saviors. But they revealed their true colors as conquerors by forcing the proud Chinese to show their submission by wearing their hair in pigtails and adopting Manchurian clothing styles. Many fought back, but within 35 years, all of China was firmly under Manchu control.

They lost no time in removing the old Ming cliques, replacing them in official posts with scholars who had been driven underground in the years of Ming rule. The new rulers placated the gentry by guaranteeing their estates, and driving out the rebels who threatened them, and this dynasty was, if anything, more single-minded than its predecessors in building elaborate palaces and temples. The conquerors also completely patterned their government on time-honored Chinese principles. The emperor was considered answerable to no one. He was ensconced within the guarded Forbidden City at Beijing, which was thought of as the center of the universe, as the ruler's surroundings had been since ancient times. Anyone privileged to have an audience with the emperor was not permitted to look on his face, but instead obligated to kowtow in his presence, bowing low enough to touch the floor with the head; and his name was forbidden to be uttered by any of his subjects.

None of these things were new to the Chinese, but though the Qing emperors adopted Chinese ritual and belief, they kept many of their Manchu customs as well. They claimed to be the saviors of Chinese culture, but they kept themselves and their countrymen slightly above the people they had saved. The same social distinctions still existed, but a new layer was added at the top. Manchu nobility was held more important than Mongol, who were a considered a cut above the native Chinese. The common people were subdivided into three classes with the peasants, who accounted for more than 80 percent of the population, above artisans, who themselves were considered slightly better than the merchant class, the lowest of the low. Status had nothing to do with income: some merchants accumulated large fortunes, but when it came to such things as marriage or legal matters, they were no better than street peddlers and had fewer rights than simple farmers.

The basis of all Qing laws went directly back to the age-old Chinese belief in family values, and often enforcement was handled in the family unit itself. The rules were simple: the older generation was superior to the younger, as men were to women. A son or a wife who accused an older man of any crime was very likely to be the one punished for it. But the eldest male in a family wasn't without his own superiors. There were ancestors to be considered and an offense against them was the worst crime of all. Family units were bound together into powerful clans with other families sharing the same ancestors. A single clan might have thousands of members in every social class, and some entire villages were run by them. The clans settled family disputes, provided financial help when it was needed and supported any member's effort to move up in the social order. They encouraged education, and provided the means when it was necessary. Some clans even ran their own schools.

Women, who had very little status in Imperial China, automatically became members of their husband's clan when they married. It was expected of every young person to get married, and no one was considered an adult until they did. The union was usually considered a joining of two families rather than just of two persons, and arrangements were always made by the older generation. In some families, especially among peasants, marriage arrangements were made for very young children, who were raised with their future spouses as brother and sister until they reached the suitable age, usually sixteen for boys and fourteen for girls.

Matchmakers handled the details in every case, the rituals including consultations with the ancestors of both families for guidance and with astrologers for proper timing. The matchmaker also negotiated the amount of money the groom's family should pay to the bride's. It was the direct opposite of the Western concept of a bride's family paying a dowry. But the idea stemmed from the fact that a girl's father had fed and clothed her and was entitled to some return on his investment.

Once all the details were settled and an auspicious day agreed upon, the groom's family sent a red sedan chair to the bride's home, and after a ritual parting with her family, she was carried through the streets to her new home and what was often her first glimpse of her new husband. More rituals were observed and the ceremony was crowned by a banquet celebrating the transfer. In most cases, the bride's family was not among the guests, though they were sometimes given a banquet of their own at the time of paying bride money and delivering gifts. The cost of all banquets connected with a wedding were borne by the invited guests.

Once the ceremonies were over, the woman was no longer connected to her original family in any way. And among the problems she faced in her new life with complete strangers was a mother-in-law, invariably the dominant member of the household. A son was bound by tradition to respect the wishes of his mother, and by inference, so was his wife. There were very few grounds for divorce by women and several rules that often made it impossible. There were more allowable reasons for men to give up their wives, ranging from a woman's inability to bear children to her tendency to talk too much, but divorce was rare. Women resigned themselves to their fate and most patiently waited for the day when they would be some other woman's mother-in-law.

The purpose of marriage among the Chinese was to produce male offspring to continue the family line. In the 265 years of the Qing Dynasty the population of China quadrupled to well over 400 million. The threat of devastating floods, which had cost so many lives in the past, was reduced through government-sponsored flood control projects. There were no serious wars, and medical advances were adding years to people's lives. The government had passed laws against emigration, which compounded the problem of overpopulation. New farming techniques helped keep the food supply high enough to feed everyone, but at the same time they also reduced the number of people required to produce it. Farmers moved off the land and into villages and cities, and the Chinese began to depend more on the merchant class than ever before.

Foreign trade became important to the Chinese economy in the early years of the 17th century, and in 1689, after a short territorial war with the Russians, the Chinese negotiated their first treaty with a foreign power. It was revised 40 years later to allow the Russians to set up a trade office, a legation and a Christian church in Beijing. It was followed two years later by a similar agreement that allowed Moslems to establish a legation as well. The Chinese had been allowing such foreign enclaves for centuries, and welcomed the strangers into their midst because in the past they had always paid tribute to the Imperial Court. But times had changed and the Chinese hadn't noticed.

The Russians, and other European powers that followed them to the Chinese capital, had a different idea of what their new treaties meant. To them they represented diplomatic equality and a trade opportunity among equals. The Chinese, of course, didn't believe any culture was equal to theirs.

They managed to keep the Europeans in their place for more than a century. And by 1800, when the

British, French, Dutch, Spanish and Portuguese had well-established Asian colonies, the Chinese had restricted their contacts to trade only through Guangshou (Canton). They were allowed to trade only at pre-determined times and only through officially sanctioned wholesalers. They sold the Westerners porcelain, tea and silk, but they imported nothing, considering Western-produced goods inferior. European gold and silver poured into China, seemingly never to return.

It was the British who figured out how to reverse the drain. They began selling opium to the Chinese. It was a disaster for China on two levels. Hard money began pouring out of the country and its citizens were becoming hopelessly addicted to the drug. In a desperate attempt to fight back, the Chinese declared war on England. But the 1839-42 Opium War was fought on Chinese soil and went badly for them. The peace treaty that ended it opened the door all the way for the English and for other European countries as well. Four more ports were open to foreign trade and soon the outsiders were spreading their influence inland as well. As part of the agreement that ended the war, the British received the port of Hong Kong (which will become part of the People's Republic of China in 1997), and other reparations, including a clause that gave Great Britain any rights the Chinese might subsequently grant to any other Western power. The war also transformed Shanghai from a small town to an international city, favored by the Europeans because of its access hundreds of miles inland on the Yangtse River. After the city surrendered to British warships it was divided up among several European powers, who declared themselves immune from Chinese laws and barred native Chinese from using the city for their own trade.

There was little cooperation between the Europeans and the Chinese, and tension between them kept growing. In 1860 a British force marched on Beijing and forced the Emperor to leave. The result was yet another treaty that legalized the British opium trade and allowed for the establishment of an English legation in Beijing. Most important to the Chinese was that the new rules also allowed for duty-free imports of European merchandise. Combined with aggressive selling by the foreigners that convinced the Chinese they really couldn't do without the imports, it created a new cash drain, and eventually the Chinese were forced to borrow from the West to pay the country's debts. The Chinese standard of living went steadily downhill and the government was faced with a series of uprisings, the likes of which its predecessors had never known.

There were other outside troubles to deal with as well. The Russians extracted Chinese territory in northern Manchuria and the Japanese took Korea from under Chinese influence. The Chinese were powerless to stop either of them because they had refused to modernize their fighting machine. But westernization had never been in the Chinese scheme of things. Any probability that they might change their ways was put aside in 1875 when the Emperor died without an heir. His three-year-old nephew was designated his successor, but when he actually took over in 1899, both he and the government were solidly under control of the Empress Dowager Tzu Hsi. She was convinced that nothing had changed in China, and therefore not in the world. Many of her advisors felt that China was in danger of becoming a European colony as so many of her neighbors had, and pointed out to Tzu Hsi that people like the Japanese, for centuries considered among the lowest of the barbarians, were now able to defeat China in a war.

The Empress Dowager ignored their dire predictions, and when they were able to convince the Emperor that it was time to reform things, she had many of them executed and the young Emperor himself imprisoned. However, when a secret society known as the Boxers began rebelling against foreigners in their midst, Tzu Hsi recruited them to join her armies in driving them out.

The Boxers believed they had magic powers that made them invulnerable to bullets, which made them fearless in the face of Western-style defenses. Their beliefs were almost exactly the same as the Ghost Dancers of the Paiute Indians in North America who were making the final effort to stop foreign annexation of their territory at the same time. Their fate was the same, too. When the Boxers killed the German Ambassador in Beijing, an international army marched on the city and saved the foreign legations from total destruction. In the process they debunked the myth of Boxer invulnerability.

Before the smoke cleared, the Empress Dowager had taken the Emperor and fled from the city in disguise. She returned in 1902, put the Emperor back into his prison and announced reforms, which were half-hearted and never enforced. She became ill six years later, at the age of 74. Sensing that she was about to die, she had the Emperor executed and named his two-year-old nephew his successor. The boy abdicated in less than four years after anti-Manchu uprisings, which began at Wuchang in October, 1911, spread throughout the country.

The father of the 1911 revolution and the Chinese Republic that grew out of it was Dr. Sun Yatsen, a man educated abroad in the Anglican tradition, with no background of Confucian thought. His new republic didn't last long, and in 1916 the government was taken over by a succession of warlords. When World War I broke out the Chinese had sided with the Allies, and when it was over they found their country virtually controlled by the Japanese, who had driven the Germans out, but kept the Chinese territory they had occupied for themselves. Anti-Japanese feeling among the Chinese weakened the Beijing government, giving new strength to Sun Yatsen's Guomindang Party, which by then had elevated its founder to the post of Generalissimo, with the goal of spreading its influence to the north from its base at Guangzhou.

The party had changed its goals over the years, and had joined with the fledgling Communist Pary in calling for reform along socialistic lines. When Sun Yatsen died in 1925, his successor, Chiang Kaishek, found Russian advisors in his midst reorganizing his armies. The Guomindang's military successes took them as far north as the Yangtze River and they moved their capital to Nanjing in 1928. By then the Communists and the Nationalists had come to a parting of the ways. When Chiang's army took Shanghai in 1927, he chose to curry favor among the capitalists there and executed his Russian advisors and about 5,000 Communist sympathizers. Among the leaders who escaped his purge was Mao Zedong, who went into hiding in the mountains straddling the provinces of Hunan and Kiangsi.

Mao gathered his followers around him and attempted several unsuccessful uprisings. Chaing Kaishek's People's Revolutionary Army responded vigorously and they finally succeeded in driving Mao and some 100,000 of his followers on the so-called Long March, which began on October 15, 1934. The journey of 6,000 miles took a year, Mao's army crossing 18 mountain ranges and 12 provinces, and fighting the Guomindang for most of the way. Only one in twenty of those who started survived, but the march brought both the message and the dedication of the Communists to the attention of the peasants, and when they finally settled at Yan'an in Shensi, Mao's army had found not only a new headquarters, but a new lease of life as well.

At the end of 1936, when war with Japan seemed imminent, a very uneasy truce was made between the two sides to present a united front against the invaders. Neither side trusted the other and they never were a united fighting force. Once the Second World War was won, the rift between the two Chinese factions quickly erupted into a civil war that ended in 1949 in a Communist victory that created the People's Republic of China. Chiang Kaishek's Nationalist Army was allowed to retreat to Taiwan, where he established what he called the "Central Government of China." He was joined by some two million of his countrymen.

In his first speech as the new leader of China, Mao Zedong blamed the country's troubles on "oppression and exploitation by foreign imperialism and domestic reactionary government." He promised that the Chinese people would no longer be insulted or humiliated: "The Chinese have stood up." he said. It was a message they were eager to hear. As the Communists systematically brought all of the mainland under their control, their effort to bring basic honesty on every level, from the smallest villages to the biggest cities, impressed the people that the message was much more than just empty rhetoric.

The Chinese allied themselves with the Soviets, but the support they received from Russia was less than generous. There was a traditional distrust between the two peoples, and Soviet Premier Josef Stalin especially distrusted the new Chairman of the Chinese Communist Party. The Americans, deep in a cold war with the Communists, had chosen to support Chiang Kaishek's Guomindang to the tune of some $6 billion (compared to about $300 million in Soviet aid to the other side). When the Communists finally took over, with the help of American equipment captured from Chiang's forces, the American government refused to recognize the new regime. It told the world that a "bamboo curtain" had been drawn around the most populous nation on earth.

The curtain parted a little in 1950 when American troops fighting in North Korea moved close to the Chinese border and were repulsed by a Chinese army. The armistice that was signed three years later was considered by Mao's followers a kind of revenge for past humiliations inflicted on China by Westerners. It stirred a new Chinese nationalism and support for the new regime as nothing else might have.

The job of rebuilding the country began with a series of five-year plans after 1955. In 1958, the party called for a "Great Leap Forward," an ambitious program that included the creation of communes to help overcome problems of food production for a country whose population was accurately predicted to double in the next 35 years. The plan was less than successful, leading to some soul-searching at Beijing, and the beginning of a rift between the Chinese and the Soviets. By 1960, when a severe drought was followed by catastrophic floods, China was on the brink of disaster. The Chinese capacity for hard work helped turn the situation around, but the perceived failure of the Great Leap had weakened Mao Zedong's position. Among his concerns was that the young Chinese who had never fought a war nor experienced humiliation at the hands of the hated foreigners might eventually turn against him and welcome outsiders, including Chiang Kaishek, back into China.

In 1966 Mao met the problem head-on with what he called a "Cultural Revolution." It began with the formation of the Red Guards, student groups that appeared almost overnight in every major school in the country. Their mandate from Beijing was to continue the revolution and promulgate the teachings of Chairman Mao, and they went at it with single-minded enthusiasm, often beating their teachers to death for their opposing views. In the months that followed, thousands of books were burned, priceless works of art destroyed, religious symbols desecrated and an estimated 35,000 people killed. Even the party faithful weren't safe from attack. In fact, they quickly became the principal targets of the Cultural Revolution. Many who had been with Mao on the Long March were forced out of office and humiliated in kangaroo trials that ended in death for some and imprisonment for the rest.

The fires began to cool in the late 1960s, and major reforms intended to adapt education to the needs of society as a whole were put into place in most parts of the country. Schools that had been closed for three years were reopened again and the reign of terror seemed to be over. In 1969, former Minister of Defense Lin Biao was named as Mao's future successor. But the revolution wasn't over yet. Lin's supporters in the military reportedly were planning Mao's overthrow, and when an actual attempt on the Chairman's life was suspected, four influential generals were immediately arrested. Lin Biao and his family escaped, but were killed in a plane crash, allegedly on their way to Russia. Credit for outsmarting the plotters went to Chairman Mao, of course, but also to Premier Zhou Enlai, whose influence had cooled the passions of the Cultural Revolution.

Among the reasons behind Lin's bid for power was opposition to an attempt by both Mao and Zhou to isolate the Soviet Union by forming an alliance with the United States. Mao surprised the world in 1970 by inviting Richard Nixon to Beijing, and on February 21, 1972, the American President arrived on Chinese soil, clearing the way for normalizing relations between the two countries. Later that same year, the People's Republic of China became a member of the United Nations, an advantage that formerly had been denied them by American influence.

In the months that followed, Zhou Enlai was hospitalized and his former protege, Deng Xiaoping was named acting premier. Deng was among the officials who had been exiled during the Cultural Revolution, and his reappearance provided a signal for the return of other survivors. Most of them were welcomed back into the government in the same jobs they had been driven from. But their troubles weren't over yet. When Zhou died, Chairman Mao announced that his successor would not be Deng Xiaoping, but the relatively unknown Hua Guofeng, and when Mao himself died eight months later, on September 9, 1976, Hua was made premier. Deng had been exiled for a second time by then, but the people themselves were clamoring for his return. They saw him as a representative of the final end of the Cultural Revolution and believed that through him they could get on with their lives. In less than a year, Deng was brought back to Beijing and restored to the posts he had held before, making him third in the order of leadership. Hua was forced to resign in 1980 and was replaced by Zhao Ziyang, a close ally of Deng's. The resignation was followed in a few months by the public trial of the so-called Gang of Four, a name

given by Chairman Mao to four of his associates he had accused of starting the Cultural Revolution for their own profit. With their conviction, China breathed a collective sigh of relief that the Cultural Revolution was finally a thing of the past. Deng himself told the people that there was no social difference between people engaged in mental and physical labor and that intellectuals were as dedicated to socialist principles as anyone. Then he invited both groups to join together in a "second revolution." He called on them to push for "Four Modernizations," encompassing agriculture, defense, science and industry.

The cities of China, created to be impressive, have been altered drastically in the modernization process. Wide boulevards, super highways, skyscrapers, luxury hotels, and factories are among the 20th-century encroachments that make many Western visitors feel right at home. But it is the people who make their homes in cities like Beijing and Shanghai that make the most lasting impression. Some 200 million Chinese live in tightly-packed city neighborhoods and are considered the elite of the new society, compared to their 800 million country cousins. Most of the city-dwellers have factory jobs, thought to be more secure and often carrying more benefits than administrative jobs, the traditional goal in other societies.

Officially, the government's policy is weighted in favor of the agricultural class, which produces the food the country desperately needs (farming occupies four out of five Chinese), but China is also pouring its resources into the production of consumer goods. The program is providing both work for city-dwellers and also luring new people from the countryside in search of a better life.

By Western standards, Chinese factory life may not be very much better than in Western cities, but it is far superior to those conditions under which pre-war manufacturers expected the Chinese to work. Then, during the Thirties, even children would work a twelve-hour day, sleeping under the machines they tended. Now the average factory worker puts in an eight-hour day, with a break for lunch in a factory canteen and sometimes a nap break in the afternoon. Most of them live in factory-supplied housing, a short bike ride away. The factories are also generous with child-care facilities and medical benefits and frequently reward good workers with the right to pass their jobs on to their children. Most belong to unions, which provide special courses aimed at advancement, as well as excursions and entertainment programs. As union members, Chinese factory workers are allowed to strike, but the law that allows it also specifies that strikes may not disrupt production.

Women, who enjoy more equality in China today than at any other time in history – and considerably more than in many Western countries – are encouraged to work, and women are frequently found in what

Western industrialized countries would consider to be traditionally male jobs in heavy industry. Many of those with small children work in collectives, small workshops and other enterprises where after-tax profits are split among the workers. Most of the collectives, which often provide jobs for young people who can't be absorbed into state-run heavier industries, are supervised by neighborhood committees, themselves very much like the family clans of the imperial era. The committees work in the same ways as the party officials who keep their eye on things in the big factories. They are there to praise the productive, scold the sluggards and make sure that the party line gets down to the lowest levels. They also provide help when it is needed by anyone in the neighborhood, from retirees to children.

Children are expected to go to school, and most do, working an eight-hour day like their parents. In their free time they are encouraged to keep busy in so-called children's palaces, learning crafts and developing artistic skills. At the other end of the scale, people who have retired find they have less to do. Because of the size of the labor force, men leave their jobs at 60, and women at 50. Factory workers are paid 90 percent of their former wage in the form of pensions, but those with no children to help support them are often retired at full pay. Many retire to the countryside, but those with grandchildren usually stay in the cities, where they make themselves useful by providing a babysitting service. The rest spend endless hours in parks reading and reminiscing.

Tradition in China gives special status to the very young and the very old. In the imperial era, children under the age of two were completely indulged. They were fed at the slightest sign of hunger and played with during every waking hour. The attention was decreased gradually over the next dozen years, a time when respect and obedience were taught. By the age of sixteen, they were considered young adults and knew they were expected to behave that way. All through their lives they were kept aware of the importance of health and longevity. And they knew there would be a reward at the end.

Throughout Chinese history, birthday celebrations have never been quite as important as those after the fiftieth, and each successive one became more elaborate than the last. At home, the elderly were as pampered as they were respected, and they were appropriately honored in public places as well.

Many of the old ideas have been abandoned, but one of the traditional roads to a long life is the enjoyment of good food, and the Chinese are still passionate about it, with the result that even France may take a back seat to the cuisines of China. Some of the credit may belong to Confucius, who wrote extensively about food and taught that nothing should be eaten that is cut crookedly or prepared without the proper seasoning. And he said nothing should

ever be overcooked. That, above all, is at the heart of Chinese cooking, but it as much related to a shortage of fuel as to the writings of a philosopher. The basis of many dishes is small chunks of meat and vegetables, quickly fried over a hot, but brief, fire. As the food was pre-cut, the ancient Chinese found it was much easier to eat with chopsticks than knives and forks, which emerged in the West to accommodate heavier eating styles.

Due to a history of chronic food shortages, the Chinese have learned to eat everything available, and some of the ingredients of a Chinese banquet seem odd to Westerners, though quite delightful to those among them willing to sample such things as bird's nest soup, camel's pads and fish lips. As their fields are terraced for better production of rice, the Chinese have little land left over for grazing, with the result that dairy products are rare. And the result of that, combined with an emphasis on fresh vegetables lightly cooked, makes Chinese cuisine unusually healthy. The fact that few Chinese are overweight is not as much a result of not having enough to eat as of eating the right things.

Every meal in China is a kind of celebration. But no celebration is quite as eagerly anticipated as the New Year festival, which always occurs at the beginning of the second full moon after the first day of winter. The date can be anywhere between January 20 and February 20, but every man, woman and child in China knows the exact date each year long in advance, almost by instinct. Preparations for it begin about two weeks ahead of the date. There is shopping to be done because families get together for three days of feasting, including the families of shopkeepers. Houses need to be thoroughly cleaned to welcome the New Year. And on the night before the first day of the celebration it is customary to stay awake to wait for the sunrise. In many households where old customs are still observed, the doors and windows of the house are sealed for the night and then ceremoniously opened as the gate to fortune. Outside, incense and evergreen branches are burned to keep evil spirits away, and firecrackers set off to frighten demons.

Part of the experience of the New Year's feast for many Chinese, especially peasants, is that they eat pork – possibly for the only time of the year. They consider it the finest of all delicacies. The rest of the time, peasants live on a diet of noodles, rice, bean curd and vegetables, with an occasional egg and possibly some chicken or fish.

Life for China's farmers has changed very little over the centuries, except for occasional evenings in a local meeting hall to discuss what is expected of them by their leaders. It is generally what was expected of their ancestors in imperial days: to make the land more productive. And it is a big job. It takes the labor of four farmers to feed their own families with enough left over to supply one factory worker. The work gives the farmers a certain amount of independence. They know they can feed their own families, come what may, and they can let them grow beyond the official limit of one child, unthinkable in the cities. Nowadays they are also allowed to own their own land. And they don't have to deal with aristocratic landlords as their ancestors did.

Farmers work from sunrise to sunset in China, just as they do everywhere else in the world. They don't have the advantage of heavy mechanization, which means they work harder themselves. But though the Chinese have a centuries-old reputation for their capacity for hard work, Western visitors are usually surprised to find an unusually slow pace among their hosts. The Chinese prefer to move slowly for the same reason that birds spend more time resting than flying. They move at a rate that conserves energy. The system has something to do with it, too. Jobs are hard to find, few workers have a real choice as to the work they are assigned to do, and even fewer entertain dreams of moving on to better positions. But when they need to, these people are capable of performing miracles. They can change the courses of rivers if such a thing is needed, and they still have the qualities that could change the course of history.

Possibly the biggest change of all has been the transformation of a closed society into one that welcomes foreigners with open arms. And the whole world is richer for it. The door has opened slowly in the first decades, but that is more the result of strained facilities than a lack of enthusiasm and pride. In the early 1970s, only 40 Chinese cities and historic sites were open for tourism. In less than ten years, the number grew to 257, including 120 cities, and it is growing still. When tourism became a way of life in China, packaged tours included factories and communes and government institutions on their itineraries. But in the years since, the emphasis has changed to include museums and historical monuments, and workrooms specializing in arts and crafts. The official government guide for tourists to China says that every visitor "will have at least a half day to visit the Friendship Stores, which offer virtually everything China produces, from embroideries, silk goods, crocheted articles and porcelain to ceramics, rubbings, tracings and toys." Interesting words, considering they come from a Communist officialdom, but a practical idea nonetheless. Forty percent of China's estimated $1.6 billion in tourist income is from the sale of souvenirs and gifts.

Yet the best souvenir any visitor can find in China is probably memories of the people. For almost a century after the West began casting lustful eyes on China's resources in 1840, they were hidden behind an age-old veil of mystery. Now the veil has been parted and anyone with even a basic curiosity can see into the future after only a few days in China. No country on earth has a bigger labor potential, and none has as many people accustomed to working for small rewards. They have an abundance of natural resources, too, especially important when compared to the Japanese, who accomplished an industrial miracle with none, and with only a fraction of the number of people.

The Chinese culture has seen world-dominating empires come and go. They have kept their ideas intact through centuries of change, and now they are on the threshold of adapting those ideas to the 21st century. Many tourists to China still think of the people as quaint, childlike and charming. Few think of them as a force that can change the world. But the force is there.

China is often perceived by outsiders as an emerging nation. In fact, the concept of a Third World consisting of undeveloped countries neutral in the East-West alignment was first put forward by Mao Zedong. But China isn't in the same category as the new nations of Africa or the underdeveloped countries of South America. It is the oldest continuing civilization in the world and doesn't feel it needs any advice from other countries. The Chinese long for Western technology, but not Western ideas. The basic concepts of Confucianism and family solidarity have been officially swept away. But class distinctions have gone, too, and China has been industrialized faster than any nation in the history of the world. The people are better educated, better fed and more directly involved in the running of their country than ever before in their history.

And although the past has become less important to the Chinese as they rush toward fulfilment of their ambitious modernization plans, the past is still very much with them. They are as much aware of their heritage as they are optimistic about their future. In their souls, the Chinese still believe in the harmony of nature. They still believe that the universe has neither a beginning nor an end and that, whatever their difficulties, in time they will prevail. No one who visits them comes away with the slightest doubt about that.

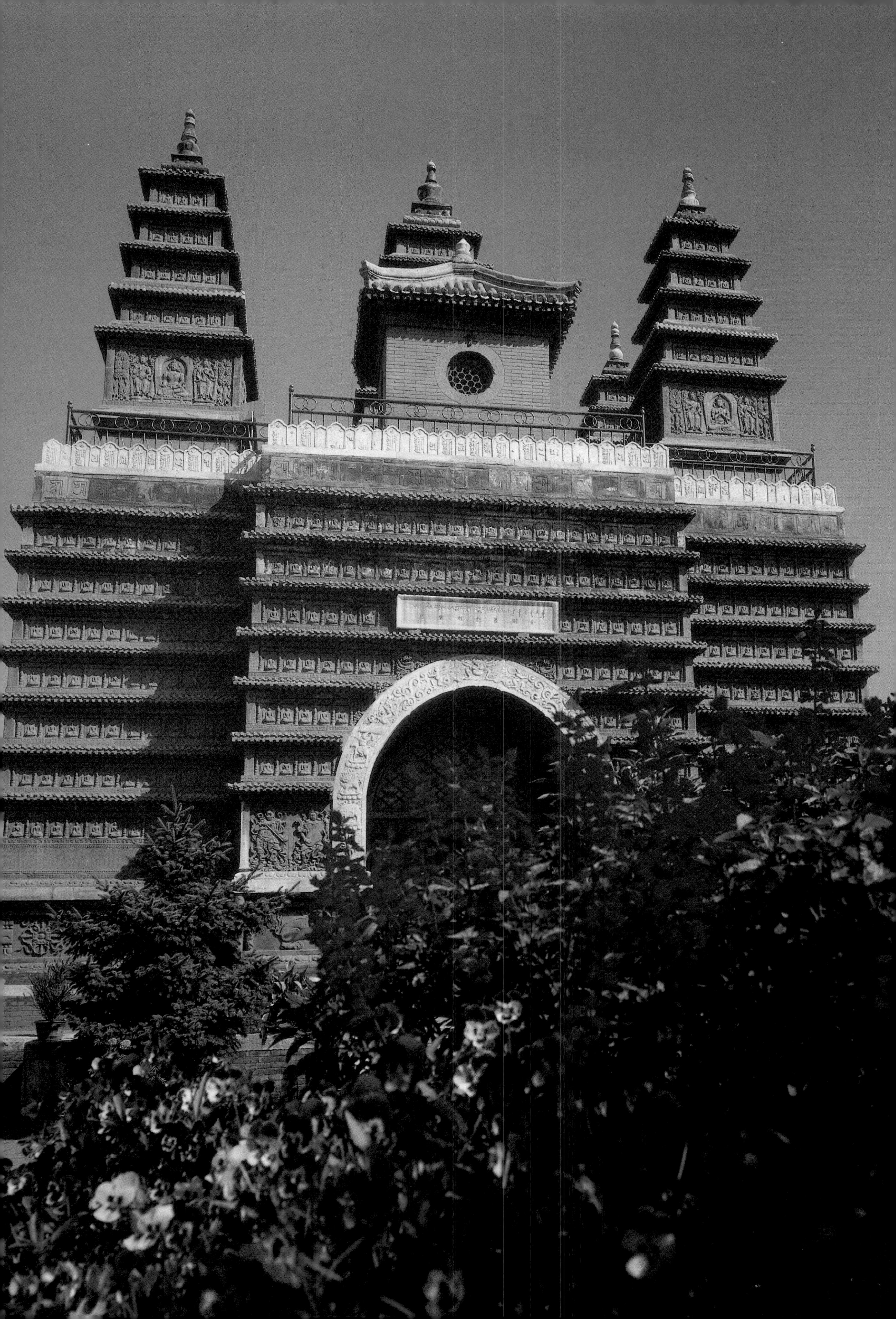

*Previous pages: Five Pagoda Temple, the only remains of the once-grand Cideng Monastery of the Qing Dynasty, just south of the People's Park in Hohhot. Right: the Tomb of Wang Zhaojun – also known as the Green Tomb – seven miles southwest of Hohhot, the capital of Inner Mongolia. The site, which is decorated with flower gardens and pergolas, commemorates a Chinese princess of the Han Dynasty, whose marriage to the King of Mongolia in the first century B.C. did much to secure friendly relations between the peoples either side of the Great Wall. Overleaf: a semi-circle of waterfalls cascading into Jingpo Lake, in northern Heilunkiang.*

16

*Left: a ribbon of white water brightens a landscape of subdued grays and greens in the Changbai Mountains, a range spanning the provinces of Kirin and Liaoning in northeastern China. Overleaf: Mount Baita, at nearly 9,000 feet the highest peak in northeastern China.*

Beiling Tomb (top) is one of several significant buildings in Shenyang, the capital of Liaoning province. It was built for Emperor Huang Taiji, the founder of the Qing Dynasty, and is the best-preserved of its era. Above: a bathing beach at the port town of Dalian, which is situated on the tip of the Liaoning Peninsula. Facing page: Mount Fengkuang, northwest of Dandong.

*Above: a sixth-century Sui Dynasty bridge and buildings, whose elegant curves seem to temper their rugged surroundings on Mount Cangyan in Jingxing County, Hopeh. Top: mid-water pavilions at the eighteenth-century Imperial Summer Retreat in Chengde, Hopeh, which also includes the remains of the largest royal gardens in China. Facing page: the huge bronze Buddha at sixth-century Longxing Monastery, at Zhengding.*

27

*The Temple of Heaven (below), a unique and beautiful structure, has become one of the symbols of China. Though the temple, which marks the sacred spot in Beijing where the emperors used to pray for a good harvest, reaches over a hundred feet in height, it was built without the aid of nails or mortar. Right: the Grand View Garden, Beijing. Bottom: the superb Nine Dragon Screen in Beijing's Beihai Park. Overleaf: the great Meridian Gate of Beijing's Forbidden City, beyond which many Chinese emperors rarely ventured.*

The magnificent Summer Palace (above and facing page top), built during the Qing dynasty as a
summer retreat, occupies a beautiful site by the shores of Lake Kunming, just seven miles
northwest of Beijing. The palace, now a popular recreational area, boasts attractions such as the
Temple of Buddhist Virtue (above) and the Seventeen-Arched Bridge (facing page top). Facing
page bottom: the Round City, in Beijing's Beihai Park. Overleaf: the huge copper Buddha that is
the centerpiece of the Temple of the Sleeping Buddha in the Western Hills.

*The Temple of the Azure Clouds (facing page), situated near the north gate of Western Hills Park, just outside Beijing, is one of the region's most significant sites. The original temple, constructed in 1366, was expanded in the eighteenth century. Above: ruins of Beijing's Summer Palace, located only a short distance from the Western Hills. Top: the tranquil lake that covers much of Beijing's Beihai Park. Overleaf: a restored section of the Great Wall of China at Badaling, northwest of Beijing.*

*The Aquatic Park (above), in the city of Tientsin – China's third largest city – is an ideal place to escape the city heat in summer. In winter its lakes make fine skating rinks. Facing page: Mount Panshan, reputed to be the most beautiful mountain east of the national capital.*

*Mount Taishan (left), the most revered of China's five holy mountains, has been commemorated by Chinese writers and poets throughout the ages. Though the climb to the summit of the mountain – some 6,000 steps in total – is a long and arduous one, the view is well worth the effort.*

Jinan, the capital of Shantung province, was once renowned for over a hundred springs, but many of these are now dry. Parks have been established round the springs that remain, such as Round-the-City Park (above) and Batou Spring Park (facing page top). Facing page bottom: Daming Lake, whose name means "gleaming brightness." The reflection of a full moon here is one of the sights of Jinan. Overleaf: nightfall silhouettes Huilan Pavilion at the end of Qingdao Pier.

*The tomb of Emperor Qin Shihuang, located on the plain outside Shensi province's capital Xi'an, is guarded by the world-famous terra cotta army (above). Remarkably, each warrior in the 6,000-strong army is different. Facing page top: Coiling Dragon Ridge on Huashan Mountain, a sacred peak in Shensi province. Facing page bottom: Huaqing Pool, near Xi'an.*

The forty-four-foot-high Sakyamuni Buddha (left) is one of the most spectacular of 50,000 Buddhist statues and bas-relief carvings to be found at the Yungang Grottoes near Datong in Shansi province. Carved out of the northern slope of Mount Wuzhou more than 1,500 years ago, these statues — each with a different expression — are among the oldest examples of stone sculpture in China. Above: Xijia Pagoda at Fogong Temple, a two-hundred-and-twenty-foot-high wooden structure in Yingxian, Shansi province. Overleaf: the Hanging Monastery in the Heng Mountains, Shansi province.

*The group of 108 conical brick pagodas (above) arranged in the shape of a great triangle, located southwest of Qingtongxia, must be one of the strangest sights in Ninghsia province. The significance of the group, and the reason for its special positioning on the upper reaches of the Huang He, or Yellow River, has been a puzzle for over 600 years. Facing page: the Union Tablet, an example of urban Revolutionary sculpture in Yinchuan, capital city of Ninghsia.*

*Facing page top: romantically-named Crescent Moon Spring, a small desert lake in the environs of Dunhuang, in Kansu province. These vast sand dunes are the start of a seemingly infinite stretch of the Kansu Desert to the southwest of the oasis town of Dunhuang. To the southwest of Dunhuang a Han Dynasty watchtower, still visible today above the tides of sand, marked the route for the camel caravans at Yangguan Pass (facing page bottom). Such caravans are still in use in the Tengger Desert (above) in the Ninghsia region.*

*The Mogao Caves (above) near Dunhuang, in Kansu province, are among the greatest archaeological finds of the East. The fourth-century Buddhist cave temples, set in the sandstone cliff face, were rediscovered in 1900. Since then extensive renovation has been undertaken and over 400 of the caves have been opened. Facing page top: Jiuquan Park, Kansu. Facing page bottom: Lanzhou, the capital of Kansu province and the second-largest city in the northwest. Overleaf: the Maijishan Grottoes in the southeast of Kansu province near Tianshui.*

Ta'er Monastery (these pages) near Xining, the capital of Tsinghai province, is the most important lamasery outside Tibet – the current Dalai Lama was born and trained here – and as such it attracts a constant stream of pilgrims. Ta'er was built in 1588 and grew into a sizeable complex with four colleges, many chapels, stupas and tombs. The monks are renowned for their elaborate yak butter sculptures of human figures, animals and even landscapes. Overleaf: saline Tsinghai Lake, the largest lake in China, which in ancient times was known as the Western Sea. An island on the lake, known appropriately as Bird Island, is a breeding ground for the rare black-necked crane.

*Lake Hanas (right) lies over 7,000 feet above sea level at the southern foot of Mount Altay, in northwestern Sinkiang. Overleaf: a ferry-boat cruises the region's startlingly-beautiful Tianchi Lake, or "Pool of Heaven," which lies amid the Tian Mountains to the east of Ürümqi.*

*The fifteenth-century Pagoda of the 10,000 Buddhas (above), otherwise known as the Kumbum, in Gyantse, Tibet, is a superb feat of architecture. It has nine tiers, is capped with gold, and from all four sides the eyes of the Buddha regard you, symbolic of his cognisance of all mankind. Facing page and overleaf: the magnificent seventeenth-century Potala Palace of the Dalai Lama that dominates Lhasa, the Tibetan capital. The Red Palace is the religious center, while the White Palace was the Dalai Lama's residence until his overthrow in 1959.*

*Namjagbarwa Feng (right), one of the mountains that encirlce Tibet – the "Roof of the World" – stands at over 25,000 feet, and is the highest peak in eastern Tibet. From its summit it is theoretically possible to see India, whose border with China lies only a few miles to the south. At the foot of the mountain flows the great Brahmaputra River, which irrigates most of southern Tibet. Overleaf: Mount Everest – the "Emperor of the Himalayas" – the highest, most alluring mountain in the world.*

*Although the port of Chongqing, at the confluence of the Jialing and Yangtse rivers in Szechwan province, has undergone numerous urban development programs since its industrialization, parts of the old town (above) remain to give some areas a picturesque, turn-of-the-century appearance. Facing page: elaborate decorations adorn the roof of Xiqin Guild Hall in Zigong, in Szechwan province. Overleaf: the ninety-foot-long Reclining Buddha at Baoding, northeast of Dazhu in Szechwan province, which depicts the Buddha entering the state of Nirvana.*

*Three Buddhist pagodas (above) stand in stark contrast to the blue-gray slopes behind them, their crisply-defined lines blurred in a nearby lake at Dali in Yünnan province. The largest pagoda, which reaches 230 feet in height, dates from the Tang Dynasty and is over 1,200 years old. Left: the White Pagoda, Yünnan. Overleaf: Black Dragon Pool Park in Lijiang, in Yünnan province.*

*The views of Lake Dian (above) from Dragon Gate on the Western Hills near Kunming, in Yünnan province, are superb. The ledge at Dragon Gate is only the width of two people – the most precarious of places from which to view this enormous lake. Facing page: creamy brown water forming a breathtaking waterfall in Luoping County.*

*Huangguoshu Falls (left), the largest in China and the pride of Kweichow province, are located just under a hundred miles from the capital city of Guiyang. The roar of the falls – which plunge over 200 feet into Rhinoceros Pool – can be heard long before they themselves are seen. These falls crown a region full of underground streams, gorges, caves, and waterfalls that stretches some 280 square miles across southwest Kweichow.*

*The landscape south of Guilin in Kwangs Chuang, in which Page Boy Hill (above) stands, is arguably the most inspiring in China, and is renowned throughout the world. In accordance with Chinese custom, each hill has been named – often quaintly, as in the case of Elephant Trunk Hill, but sometimes evocatively, as in Folded Brocades Hill and Embroidery Hill. Facing page top: Nanning, the sub-tropical capital city of Kwangs Chuang. Facing page bottom: the magnificent, wooden Chenyang Bridge, north of Guilin, which is constructed without a single nail. Overleaf: early morning tranquillity on the Lijiang River, in Kwangs Chuang .*

*For fifty miles of its course, between Guilin and Yangshuo in northeast Kwangs Chuang, the Lijiang River (right) is flanked by dramatically-shaped needles of eroded limestone, which rise suddenly from the flat ground. The Lijiang River flows slowly here, and is often swathed in mists, lending a languid air to the landscape. Nowhere is it more beautiful than at Yangshuo (overleaf), a tiny country town whose name means Bright Moon.*

*Farmhouses (left) huddle on the fertile valley floor at the foot of Mount Jiuyi in Hunan province. Overleaf: outcrops of rock on Hunan province's Mount Tianzi are home to trees which seem almost as light and feathery as the mists that float beside them.*

Yueyang Tower (above), an eighth-century pagoda constructed entirely without nails, is situated by the banks of the Yangtse River, at the town of Yueyang. Facing page top: Mount Heng – one of China's five holy mountains – lying south of Hunan's capital, Changsha. Facing page bottom: Aïwan Pavilion on Yuela Hill in Changsha bears a tablet of Mao Zedong's writing, for this was a haunt of the Chinese leader during his youth.

*A replica of the Yellow Crane Tower (above) at Wuhan, the capital of Hupeh province, replaces the third-century original which was burned down in 1884. It is said that the tower was built by an innkeeper in grateful memory of an Immortal who drew a magic crane on his inn wall to pay for a meal; the drawing would come to life at intervals, so attracting custom for the innkeeper. Facing page: a spectacular view of Jinxui Valley from Dragon Head Cliff on Mount Lu, near the northern border of Kiangsi province. Overleaf: the Ancestor Worshipping Cave, at Longmen Caves in Honan province.*

*Right: the Huang range of mountains in southern Anhwei. Holy Mount Huang itself is the object of pilgrimage and it is the aim of every Chinese to climb it at least once in a lifetime. Even for those indifferent to the spiritual benefits of such a climb, the almost ethereal beauty of the place turns the fulfilment of such an ambition into its own reward. Overleaf: Mount Huang in Anhwei, covered in hoar frost.*

願一心長持半偈想當年菩提樹下用何等別苦力

*Above: the rock formation known as Stone Monkey in the Huago Hills near Lianyungang, Kiangsu province. Facing page: a Buddhist statue in Roushen Hall on Mount Jiuhua, southern Anhwei. Mount Jiuhua is one of the sacred Buddhist mountains in China, and as such has been a site of pilgrimage for nearly 2,000 years.*

*The Suzhou River (top) is one of Shanghai's two waterways, the other being the larger Huangpu River. Shanghai's hectic harbor and financial center (above), known as the Bund, is situated at the confluence of the two rivers. Monumental 1930s buildings still line the Bund, evidence of Shanghai's flamboyant past. Facing page: Nine Bend Bridge in the city's sixteenth-century Yu Gardens, a haven of peace in this busy city.*

*East Lake (facing page), just outside the town of Shaoxing, is perhaps the most captivating man-made lake in Chekiang province. It was formed in a quarry of hard green rock after hill streams were dammed; steep cliffs, jade green and black with lichen and moss, border the sparkling water. Above: the ninety-foot-high Six Harmonies Pagoda at Hangzhou, in Chekiang, built 1000 years ago to ward off the spirit held responsible for the province's Qiantang River's tidal bore.*

*Above: Puji Temple, part of a Buddhist monastery on Puishan Island – an island which is sacred for Buddhists as the center of the cult of the Goddess of Mercy. Top: a magnificent Sui Dynasty pagoda, situated on Tiantai Mountain, at the watershed of the Yongjiang, Cao'e and Lingjiang rivers in eastern Chekiang province. Facing page: a Buddhist stupa in the grounds of the Xileng Seal Engravers' Club in Hangzhou, Chekiang.*

*Shuzhuang Park (above), on Gulangyu Island in Fukien province, is full of pavilions, has a walkway to the island's largest beach, and boasts one of the finest landscaped rockeries in southern China. The island itself, whose name means "Garden of the Sea," is a delightful place, being hilly and full of greenery. Facing page: stone carvings on Gu Mountain in Fuzhou, the capital city of Fukien province.*

Top: the Wuyi Mountains in western Fukien. This range is renowned both as a Buddhist retreat — over a hundred monasteries can be found on its slopes — and also for Dahongpao tea, one of the many teas produced in Fukien. Above: Xiamen and (facing page) nearby Gulangyu Island, Fukien. Both districts are lent a colonial air by the many nineteenth-century European houses that remain there today.

*The great Zhujiang River Delta (facing page), an extremely fertile region around Kwangtung, was the center of the Opium Wars of the nineteenth century. Once known as Canton, Guangzhou – the capital of Kwangtung province – is one of the liveliest cities in China and a major port, receiving ocean shipping from the South China Sea by courtesy of this deep waterway. Above: elaborate details in wood in Qinghui Gardens, Kwangtung.*

Hainan Island is the furthest limit of southern Chinese civilization, and was once a place of exile. Today it has a burgeoning tourist industry, its tropical forests and fine beaches (facing page) luring Chinese and foreigners alike. Above: Tianya Haijiao beach or "the edge of the sky and the end of the sea," at the southernmost tip of Hainan. Overleaf: the Wanquan River, which flows east from Hainan Island's central mountains.

# INDEX